The Crisis and Future of the Left

The Debate of the Decade

THE CRISIS AND THE FUTURE OF THE LEFT

Contributions by
Tony Benn, Stuart Holland, Audrey Wise
Tariq Ali, Paul Foot, Hilary Wainwright
and others

Edited by Peter Hain

Pluto Press

First published 1980 by Pluto Press Limited,
Unit 10 Spencer Court, 7 Chalcot Road, London NW1 8LH

0 86104 313 8

Cover designed by David King

Typeset by Grassroots Typeset, London NW6
Printed in Great Britain by Lowe & Brydone Ltd,
Thetford, Norfolk

Preface

This book is based upon a transcript of the debate on the future of the left held in Central Hall, Westminster, on 17 March 1980. All the main speakers have had the opportunity to correct the typed transcript and, in view of the sustained barracking some of the speakers were subjected to, a few deletions and alterations have been made so that the spoken word reads as well as is possible in print. So although it is not easy to capture the flow of the debate, its substance is presented more or less in its entirety.

We are grateful to Pluto Press for publishing it speedily so that it can usefully encourage further debate and discussion amongst socialists while the debate is still fresh in the mind. Our thanks also to Rita Moore Services for typing the transcript, to Peter Walker and Martin Lewis for arranging the recording, and for their unusual initiative of producing an LP record of the debate. This is available from the Labour Coordinating Committee, 9 Poland Street, London W1, price £1.99 plus 50p post and packing. The record is aimed at local meetings, again to provoke further discussion.

Finally, the book is dedicated to those hundreds of people who tried without success to obtain a ticket for the debate.

PETER HAIN
INQUEST ON THE LEFT

For a couple of weeks in March 1980 Nigel Stanley's phone went mad. Piles of letters came in daily and he was deluged with callers as secretary of the Labour Coordinating Committee. They all wanted one thing: tickets for the debate on 'The Crisis and Future of the Left'. It was held on the evening of 17 March and, by the previous Tuesday, all 2,600 seats had been sold. Hundreds of unsuccessful applications were returned. Members of the LCC's Executive were solicited for tickets by distant acquaintances who proffered their abiding friendship and loyalty to the working class. The switchboard of *The Times* was jammed after publication of a feature article previewing the debate. And, despite prior publicity that all seats were sold, hundreds queued outside in the wet on the night, waiting in vain for a ticket.

Why was there such enormous interest? No doubt a factor was a platform of well known and interesting speakers - Tony Benn, Paul Foot, Tariq Ali, Stuart Holland, Hilary Wainwright and Audrey Wise. But those who attended - including many who were not members of any left group - expressed the real reason: a strong desire to listen to and participate in a serious inquest into socialist ideas and strategy, springing partly from a recognition that the left no longer held all the cards it appeared to ten years ago. In 1969, when the Central Hall last echoed to the sound of argument between Labour left and far left speakers, the shop stewards movement was in the saddle; the TGWU and AUEW had new left leaders; the student movement was on the offensive. Socialism had an ideological and moral authority which bred excitement and gave reason for confidence even during the tail end of a discredited right-wing Labour government.

Now the picture is very different. Derek Robinson has been sacked with impunity; the AUEW leadership has lurched rightwards; and the trade union movement as a whole is in political disarray, unsure of its grass roots base, uncertain about its national direction; the left outside the Labour Party is weaker in terms of its political base; the student movement is passive and middle-of-the-road in its politics; and the Labour Party, whilst moving significantly leftwards, still has not shaken off a dominant right-wing leadership. Above all, socialism patently lacks the appeal and allegiance in the working class which it once had. That, as Tony Benn made clear in his contribution to the debate, is the *collective* failure of the left. The Labour Party may shoulder most of the blame - and Paul Foot's indictment is a powerful one - but the left as a whole can hardly claim to have generated a mass crusade for socialism which is being thwarted only by rightist Labour leaders.

It was against that background that the Labour Coordinating Committee decided to organise the debate. The intention was to explore the issue of left unity and not simply to reiterate existing entrenched positions. The LCC felt that the Tory offensive made sectarianism an even greater luxury than normal and that the question of unity in action ought to be discussed. However it cannot be said that the debate succeeded in that task. Partly no doubt because of organised attempts to disrupt the proceedings - and in particular the speeches of Tony Benn and Paul Foot - by self-styled 'autonomists', the debate took place in a rather sour atmosphere. Indeed, the left that night could hardly hardly have endeared itself to the unconverted.

Nevertheless, those fortunate enough to get a seat

did hear a series of clear and stimulating statements from different positions on the left, both from the platform and from the floor. There were classic critiques - by Stuart Holland of the far left; and by Paul Foot and Tariq Ali of reformism and Labour's failures. But there were also new and interesting ingredients injected into the traditional clash between 'reformists' and 'revolutionaries', by Hilary Wainwright, Tony Benn and Audrey Wise. Hilary Wainwright argued cogently the failures and shortcomings of *both* the Labour Party and centralist left groups such as the SWP or IMG, reflecting the themes of the book *Beyond the Fragments* of which she is a co-author and which sprang from the experience of the women's movement. Tony Benn chose to question the revolutionary credentials of far left groups, arguing that they too had failed and that what was required was a new socialist synthesis between parliamentary reform and rank and file struggle - an argument developed by Audrey Wise who denied any necessary conflict between pressure inside and agitation outside the system.

In that respect the terms of the debate shifted significantly from the one in 1969, and it seems a good moment to take stock, to see both how the present reactionary onslaught can be resisted and how the depressing experience of recent Labour administrations can be avoided in future. It ought first to be clear that Thatcherism's deliberate attack on the working class will not be defeated by manoeuvres in Westminster, still less by a feeble Labour opposition, hamstrung by its own record in office and without any clear socialist analysis. The Tories will only be defeated or paralysed by rank and file struggle on the shop floor and in the neighbourhood linked to national political leadership. But if we are not to see an action-replay of the 1970s - workers' agitation leading to Tory downfall (itself by no means certain), leading to an abandonment of socialist policies by Labour in office - then the labour movement requires a radical re-orientation.

There are several key elements. First, the Labour Party must end its overriding pre-occupation - not to say obsession - with electoralism and embrace extra-parliamentary struggle wholeheartedly, so that its interventions at Westminster or town hall level are underpinned by a real power base, capable of acting as a countervailing force to the extra-parliamentary powers of big business, high finance and bureaucracy that make up modern capitalism. Far left groups of course argue that it is not possible for Labour to adopt this strategy, that the party is welded to parliamentarianism in a way that inevitably encourages it to be absorbed by the ruling class. Paul Foot put this case with force in the debate. And there is a sense in which both his and Tariq Ali's argument that the Labour Party has only welcomed rank and file agitation while in opposition rings true, although they both failed to demonstrate why this should by definition be the case.

The track record of Labour's left may not be all that impressive. But then neither is that of the rest of the left - a point made with strength by Tony Benn. If we are to accept that the Labour Party is incapable of acting as the vehicle for socialist change by relying on a historical analysis, then surely similar criteria must apply for the left at large? Just one example illustrates this point: the Communist Party in the 1930s was organising in a way that groups such as the SWP are attempting today; indeed, it was doing so with greater effect and much greater support. And it is not enough to rely upon erudite distinctions in socialist ideology - between Stalinism and Trotskyism - as a major reason for anticipating greater success this time round. The plain fact is that the various left groups, the CP, SWP and IMG (not to mention their many derivatives), together enjoy substantially *less* working class backing than similar types of groups received before the second world war.

Of course, all sorts of arguments will be cited in favour of far left groups, *this* time, in *these* particular historical circumstances, facing *that* specific stage in capitalist development. But then they always are. Capitalism always is in, or approaching, its final crisis. Class conflict always is about to break out like wildfire the length and breadth of the country. The working class is perpetually about to leap up and overthrow the existing order. Indeed, some of the cruder far left groups like the WRP sustain their appeal on precisely such a diet of the revolution-just-around-the-corner. Yet a cool look at reality shows such a perspective to be illusory - and dangerously so when account is taken of the toll in terms of disillusionment expressed in the extremely high rate of membership turnover experienced by the far left, resulting very often in dropping out of political action altogether. Now disillusioning your members has not been the prerogative of far left organisations: the Labour Party has been pretty successful at it too. All that is being argued is that the balance sheet is fairly even, and that whereas there were grounds for believing at the time of the last debate between *Tribune* and the student left around *Black Dwarf* in 1969 that the far left had more attractive arguments, the experience of failure since has damaged their case, perhaps irreparably.

It was therefore of note that whilst Tariq Ali correctly emphasised that the capitalist state would not give up power voluntarily and without a fight, that classic defence of the insurrectionary strategy of revolutionary socialism was not the major argument of the far left during the debate; nor did their speakers emphasise their undoubted belief in a centrally controlled, disciplined party. Instead, Paul Foot relied considerably on the argument that serious and impact-making action needed to be at rank and file level, and that it was groups such as the SWP which intervened most effectively at that level, providing the most committed and effective activists.

But, increasingly, the radical Labour left would not quarrel with the first part of that argument, namely, the priority given to action at grass roots level. Where there would be disagreement is over the real impact of SWP-type activism. There is no question that activists in the SWP have been increasingly important on set-piece occasions like Lewisham where they can often put the rest of the left (including the CP and the Labour Party) to shame. In specific struggles like that waged by the Anti-Nazi League they have undoubtedly played a crucial role. They have also intervened relatively successfully (given their numbers) on the industrial front. But the real test lies not in an ability to mount impact-making activity in the short term: it is in sustaining a durable strategy over the long term. And on that count the far left is weak. It tends to drain the energies of its supporters in frenetic activity - another reason for high membership turnover - and to move in and out of struggles or issues. Labour Party politics may be less spectacular but it is equally far less transient. The comparison with the record of protest and community action groups during the 1970s is instructive. They too have suffered badly from an inability to sustain their momentum, partly because of a lack of resources and partly because they did not engage with the labour movement. They too have been highly successful in particular struggles lasting no more than a couple of years, thereafter frequently collapsing with their activists exhausted - a fact to which Hilary Wainwright gave scant attention in stressing the achievements of the women's movement and of community organisations.

One of the least appealing attributes of the far left is its self-righteousness: its claims to possess a monopoly on socialist wisdom, on morality and honesty, and, in the case of the SWP specifically, its irritating tendency to exaggerate its self-importance and the role of its activists. That sort of approach makes left unity difficult to build. It also reflects a fault of the whole of the left, inside and outside the Labour Party, namely, a propensity to *posture* rather than to grapple with reality. Thus the easy slogan, the reach-me-down cliché, and the obsession with sectarian pointscoring amongst the left, not a little evident in the debate. In one sense the left is its own worst enemy. And yet, when it does decide to move collectively, as we saw in the example of the Anti-Nazi League during 1977-79, it is almost irresistible, however one may qualify the ANL's success because of its limited target of the National Front.

The Labour Coordinating Committee debate therefore helped to focus on the moment of truth faced by socialists. Within our various groups we may be *organisationally* stronger - a claim made especially on behalf of the SWP. And the Labour left has undoubtedly grown in strength and influence. But against both should be counterposed the decline of the Communist Party's membership and its industrial strength. The real issue to be confronted, however, is the serious erosion of the left's political base in the working class, illustrated most vividly in voting patterns at the last general election, in the antagonism to trade unions amongst ordinary working people and in the current climate of pouplar reaction. Now it is easy to lay the blame for this on successive sell-outs by Labour MPs, councillors and trade union leaders - and there is no question that they deserve much of the criticism they get. But these by now ritual denunciations really pass the buck. The issue for us to face is how and why the left *allows* them to sell out. We cannot acquit ourselves entirely and blame the personal failings of labour movement leaders or the political shortcomings of the Labour

Party. If there really was the head of steam so frequently claimed by the left then leaders would not be allowed to sell out.

An honest assessment of the state of the left, coupled with a sensitive analysis of the nature of working class politics in contemporary Britain, shows both the purely parliamentary strategy and the insurrectionary (often now equated with rank and file) strategy to have failed. In fact, history reveals that in advanced capitalist societies such as Britain, neither strategy can succeed on its own, partly because both have misconceived the role of the state, albeit from markedly different standpoints. The insurrectionary approach views the state as unequivocally hostile to the working class, neglecting the reality that the working class has won important benefits from the modern state, such as housing, welfare, education and trade union rights. All of these have been inadequate and their concession does allow the state more effectively to exert social control whilst also facilitating the *reproduction* of the capitalist system: nonetheless they have significantly advanced working class rights and living standards. Moreover, the far left's total rejection of parliament neglects the reality that it is almost universally *seen* by the population as the legitimate, democratic vehicle for political consent and change. On the other hand, the parliamentary approach refuses to concede that parliament is only one of a series of power bases and that, by comparison with others such as the business world, civil service, the police, armed forces, and the media, its power is heavily circumscribed and in any case subject to the dictates of capitalism. Indeed, parliament is so constrained that it cannot alone tackle or control those other sources of power: to a very large extent it is placed in a straitjacket by them and thus an exclusively electoral strategy is rendered impotent.

The new Labour left recognises that (see Geoff

Hodgson, *Socialism and Parliamentary Democracy*, Spokesman 1978) and is consequently to be distinguished from the tradition of Nye Bevan and Michael Foot. Whilst acknowledging the importance of gaining a parliamentary majority to legitimate and encourage the process of change, it recognises that this will fail unless a priority is given to extra-parliamentary struggle and campaigning. For only by such struggle can the system be confronted effectively, the leadership of the labour movement be held accountable and the sources of socialist transformation be created. With that in mind the Labour left is seeking to build alliances with rank and file trade unionists, with community groups, the women's movement and with single-issue or protest campaigns, so that they can help to give new impetus to the labour movement, ultimately transforming it.

Of course it can and doubtless will be argued that the acceptance of such a strategy by the Party as a whole is by no means certain, and the far left can be forgiven a certain healthy scepticism on the matter. But events are moving logically towards its adoption, first by the Labour left and then by the movement as a whole. The Labour left is now willing to organise in a more serious way, evidenced by the activities of the Campaign for Labour Party Democracy, the LCC, ILP (and even *Militant*, though the latter's present high profile is artificial and its brand of politics sterile). An important catalyst in this process has been the pressure for extending democracy and accountability within the Party. That pressure was born out of the frustrating experience of Labour leaders repeatedly abandoning Party policies when in office. But even if and when MPs are subject to automatic re-selection, when the leader of the Party is democratically elected, when the manifesto is determined by the Party and not by an elite of MPs, the Party will *still* remain trapped within a hostile capitalist system. Internal democracy does not by itself guarantee the success of battles for socialism external to the Party, although it will enormously enhance the strength of those battles in a way the wider left has not understood. The logical next step therefore becomes to move from internal democracy to building new sources of working class power.

If that perspective is adopted then the terrain of struggle for the left will change dramatically and left unity will take on a new meaning. Instead of the Labour Party looking to Trafalgar Square solely whilst in opposition, a priority will be given to constant struggle at the base of society, fighting to remove the Tories when they occupy office and strengthening the power base of Labour Party representatives when they secure office. But we have to be clear that such a perspective requires those Party representatives to be subordinated to rank and file control. It is not a matter of having a convenient stage army to bring out when the Labour leadership deems necessary, as cynics might imagine.

Ultimately however, winning such a position for the labour movement will be a huge task and there is no question that the prospects for its achievement will be enormously strengthened both by building the left within the Labour Party and by links to independent socialist movements outside, whether political parties, trade unions, women's groups or community organisations. It is that thorny issue of building left links which this book raises and which the left at large can no longer duck.

PETER HAIN

I would like now to open the Debate on behalf of the Labour Coordinating Committee and welcome you all here. I'll just repeat my request to everybody to respect the wishes of the hall organisers: they have a no-smoking rule here and we'll have to observe that for the whole evening.

We called this 'The Debate of the Decade' - a modest title, and one which brought this comment from *The Sun*, that well known revolutionary socialist newspaper. It said: 'Health hazard warning. Left-wing MPs Tony Benn and Stuart Holland are to argue out the crisis and future of the left in London next month with others including yesterday's dreaded Tariq Ali and today's fashionable Trotskyite, the Right Honourable Paul Foot. Modestly the non-event is billed as the Debate of the Decade.' So it's on that high point that I'd like to open it and to say that we have in fact sold out, and to some extent I suppose all of us are fortunate in being here. We sold out this debate last Tuesday - which didn't stop a representative of the Pakistani Embassy queueing from 12.30 today, and when he'd been assured that he couldn't come in he sent his messenger round to queue in his place! I think that what this reflects and what this represents in the huge turn out here this evening is a thirst for real socialist argument and debate on the left.

Now what will be the order of speaking this evening? First we have Stuart Holland opening up, followed by Hilary Wainwright, followed by Paul Foot, then Tony Benn. Then we will have a period for contribution from the floor and I'll ask for everybody to fill in speakers' slips, put your name and your organisation on those slips and hand them to the stewards later on in the proceedings so that you can be called if there is time to hear you during the time for discussion. We're having to keep a very tight control on time. All the speakers have been balanced out on time and will be stopped if they go over that, just as, I'm afraid, all speakers from the floor will have to be restricted to two minutes each. We will be taking a collection at the end of the meeting - there won't be a big appeal for this but I hope you'll give generously - for the steelworkers' strike.

Applause

If you could as you go out the door simply put your contributions in - I would hope that out of an audience of 2,600 we will at least raise £1000.*

Now the theme of this debate this evening is the crisis and future of the left. It's both about the crisis of capitalism and about the crisis of the left. We have to recognise, unpalatable as it may be, that while on the one hand the Labour left is at its strongest for many years, the leadership of the Party is firmly in the control of the right wing. We have to recognise too that support for the far left groups - those groups to the left of the Labour Party, and those individuals not even in any specific political group on the left - support is in fact weaker than for many years. I think we have to recognise - and I think it's a sombre recognition - that the trade union movement, while it has gained increasing organisational and membership strength, has hardly switched to the left - the disgraceful sacking of Derek Robinson and the failure of the AUEW to stand firmly by him is, I think, testimony to that. So to some extent we are meeting in a situation of paradox, where socialism provides the only answer to the crisis of British capitalism yet at the same time popular support for socialist ideas and support for socialist movements is at

---

*In fact more than £1000 was raised.

a low ebb, for many different reasons.

Therefore I think what we have to explore this evening are not simply the arguments between us, not simply the issues which divide us, for they will remain after this debate as they will be reflected during the debate. But how we can cooperate, on what basis we can forge unity and how we can strengthen the socialist movement and move forwards, to face the crisis and the attack mounted on working-class people, from a position of strength rather than from a position of weakness. Now I am in that respect very struck by the fact that every single member of this platform - and I suppose that goes for most of the people in the meeting at large - were all active members of the Anti-Nazi League. We were all able to cooperate together, to fight together on a specific activist programme. I hope that that kind of unity might reflect itself in other movements and that we will see this evening not only a clash of ideas, not only a difference of opinion and an arguing out of those differences, but also a fraternal and comradely exchange of views that can move the left forward genuinely and firmly at this particular time. It's on that basis that I'll call Stuart Holland, the Member of Parliament for Vauxhall, Lambeth, to open up the debate. Stuart!

Applause

STUART HOLLAND

Chairman, comrades. It's not wholly clear to me whether this is *the* debate of the decade or *a* debate *for* the decade or simply a debate just into the decade. But quite clearly debate it is, and it has struck a response not only from those here tonight but those who couldn't be here because we didn't take Wembley Stadium rather than Westminster Central Hall. It also is clear that there are issues, and there is a crisis, which the thinking and self-critical left must take account of against the background of the seventies and the prospects for the eighties. This may be less a matter of learning from mistakes rather than learning in effect from experience.

The degree of working-class support for this Conservative government can be exaggerated. It is clear in fact that less than a third of new voters backed the Tories at the polls. Nonetheless, we have to face the fact that Labour last time round itself faced the electorate with no clear cut alternative and the voters could be forgiven for asking 'Which twin was the Tory?'.

The main limit of *ultra* left criticism in this case is neglect of the *radical* left within the Labour Party and labour movement through the seventies. This may be changing, and this meeting in fact may be evidence of that change. The fact is, if we focus on what we have in common, that both the ultra and radical left saw the crisis coming at both the national and international level; that both shared key insights into the coming of the second slump as evidenced by our analysis, Mandel's analysis, and your analysis, to name but a few.

But neither the ultra left, nor the radical left inside the Labour Party, and I stress that, were able to mobilise sufficient support for a radical programme in the seventies or minimise the impact of the caring cutters of public spending in Labour government as opposed to the thoroughly manic monetarists of that fraction of the Tory Party which now rules the country. The question is not simply one of tactics but also one of strategy. It relates to different conceptions of the role of the state, political power, economic power, ideas and ideology.

Now there are some, including George Matthews in today's *Morning Star*, who claim that those of us on the left inside the Labour Party are social democrats. Name games can be played as you please, but some of us have a record of criticism and opposition to the *means* of social democracy; to its reliance on indirect state intervention versus direct action; its parliamentarianism, and its basic appeasement and placation of capital. But the *ends* of at least the main post-war generation of social democrats should not thereby be derided. Housing, health, education, welfare, and the defence of public spending are crucially important for working people, as we now see by the Tory attack on them.

I'm not going to address myself to that fraction of so-called social democrats who have moved ardently to the right in the 1970s, who claim that there is an inherent limit in public spending, or who oppose planning and public enterprise. Nor do I agree with the concept of *consensus* of social democrats who compromise and mediate with the power structure as it is rather than realise that only a transformation of power through socialist policies for public spending, intervention, planning and workers' struggles can achieve the ends of social democracy. In short the crisis of the social democratic left lies substantially in its failure to realise that the aims of social democracy imply and necessitate democratic socialism.

On the other hand the ultra left, with a vision of the Vanguard Party, its concept of democratic centralism and its polarisation of reform versus revolution, have not mobilised the working class of this country as the crisis has deepened. We on the left predicted the crisis. The crisis has occurred. But spontaneous mobilisation of working people against capitalism has not occurred, and we have to admit that it has not occurred. In effect today's state and today's working class are not the same as those of 1917 or 1939. Many working people consider that the welfare *state*, however we may criticise it, and want to work for a welfare *society*, has brought major gains to working people of a kind not recognised by some of the ultra left, by, for example, this week's issue of *Socialist Challenge* or, if it comes to that, by Duncan Hallas talking of new wine in old bottles.

We have to face the fact that the state is in crisis. But we also must recognise the period of some twenty five years after the war in which it neither was patently in crisis nor coherently challenged by the democratic left. We know that it is very well to talk of workers' struggles, that it is very well to work with women in women's struggles, but the fact is that this has not mobilised a mass workers' or women's movement within the working class behind the radical left, far less behind the revolutionary demands.

We also should recognise, and I would argue this very strongly, that there is a false dichotomy between reform and revolution; that the domestic achievements of the post-war Labour government, whatever its compromise or compliance with the US in international affairs, achieved a fundamental and, until now, unreversed change in the balance of power towards working people and their families, challenged only now by this Tory government, backed by those interests of the capitalist class who hitherto were restrained by the consensus makers among the Conservatives.

We also have to take account of the fact that Gramsci was on to more than notebooks from prison when he asked the question why, with a major organisation of the working class in Italy and a developed theory of the dictatorship of the proletariat and seizure of state power, a clown such as Mussolini could lead a carnival march on Rome and seize state power - smashing the unions and the working class for a quarter of a century rather than being smashed or being seized by them.

Besides, in the last analysis, Gramsci's arguments were voiced from prison and not from a praesidium. He rightly stressed that consensus was not simply a matter of what social democrats do, but rooted in profound cultural, social and psychological values of the working class; that consent was conditioned by a degree of realism among working people, an awareness of the divorce between theory and practice of much of the revolutionary left and left rhetoric.

We no doubt will hear today something or much of Labour's programme in the seventies, including the ambition, the aim of the programme to achieve a major extension of public enterprise, real planning powers, genuine industrial democracy from the shop floor into Whitehall and the state apparatus. No doubt we shall also hear later of the failure of Labour's radical programme for the transformation of state power and the social relations of production. But if Labour's programme mainly posed the *issues* of democratic transformation of power, if the executive and conference of the Party mainly opposed the Labour government rather than held it to account, if the trade union leadership failed to transform the social contract into a contract for socialism, nonetheless the Labour Party put these issues onto the main stage of the theatre of politics in Britain today - rather than the upstage, backstage or off-stage political theatre of some of the ultra left. The struggle for power within the Labour Party now embodied in clear divisions within the party, in the conference struggles in the Party, and in the industrial struggles of the movement, is not about *whether* but *how* to implement a radical economic programme. The radical left is not divided on this key aim and I stress this. The radical left is not divided on the key aim of transforming political economic or state power. But it is part, and we must be part, of a mass movement capable of transforming rather than simply challenging that power, and as such we invite democratic socialists to join us.

Applause

Peter Hain

Thank you Stuart. I'm sure we're going to have very many different contributions this evening and some are going to express themselves in legitimate terms and some are simply going to sloganise. If you wish to do that, that's your choice, but some of us here, the majority of us are here I suspect, for a serious clash of ideas and an argument.

Applause

And on that note I'd like to introduce Hilary Wainwright who of course is co-author of what many of us feel to be a seminal work on the left, *Beyond the Fragments*. Hilary.

HILARY WAINWRIGHT

Well Stuart talked a lot about a mass movement; and indeed what distinguishes the present Labour left is the many kindly pats on the head they do give to extra-parliamentary politics, to the women's movement, to shop stewards' committees and so on. What I want to do is talk about the *direction*, the political *content* of extra-parliamentary activity. Is the extra-parliamentary activity, the mass movements to which the Labour left give support, merely like 'extra-curricular' activity, just a worthy back up to the real thing, the work that goes on in parliament, the work aimed at bringing to power a radical Labour government? Or are extra-parliamentary movements like the women's movement, some shop stewards' combine committees, tenants' groups and others *themselves* the basis for a form of new political power? Are *they* the real thing for which parliamentary activity is just one source of support?

There are a lot of Labour Party members involved in many of these extra-parliamentary movements. I want to draw their growing support for these organisations to its logical conclusion and argue that, as these extra-parliamentary movements and organisations make links between each other, as they develop policies linking their own interests to wider social needs they are themselves the beginnings of a form of political power far more democratic, far more directly accountable, and a hundred times more powerful against private capital than parliament can ever be. They are the *means*, that is the only power through which production could be socialised under popular control, and, in the ways they organise, in the values and the new ways of relating to people which they create, they give a hint of our *ends*, of the sort of society we want to create.

But that's all a bit abstract, so to illustrate the difference between the two views of extra-parliamentary activity, to show the way in which the Labour left's belief in the power of parliament conflicts with the development of this popular power, I want to tell a story from Tyneside, the story of a factory closure on Tyneside.

In January last year Dr. Stuart Holland here was economic adviser to workers at Vickers Scotswood facing the closure of their factory - this was during the Labour government. Consistent with the Labour left's belief that the existing state could exert control over the big corporations, he advised the campaign to direct its energies to getting the *government* to buy Scotswood through the NEB or to make Vickers keep the factory open. The alternative would have been for the workers to direct their energy to building up the shop stewards' combine committee which had support within most of the different plants of Vickers, to take action within those profitable plants and within the doomed factory itself, to exert power *directly* on Vickers to keep the factory open. This option of focusing the campaign more directly on Vickers wasn't put strongly. After all, thought many of the shop stewards, Stuart worked in government, he had written the industrial sections of the Labour Party manifesto, there must be something in his optimism that the pressure on the government was the best option. And they expected a Labour government to take action over a closure in an area like Tyneside. So the result was that the campaign spent its limited energies on the regular trail to Westminster week after week, lobbying the government. There was no time, no energy left to go round to Swindon, to Glasgow, to Leeds to put the argument for Scotswood, to build up the power of the combine committee.

Now the climax of all this lobbying was a tripartite meeting; a meeting where government, the unions and management sat down together to work out the problem. Now Tony Benn obviously thinks these tripartite discussions are important. He says in his collection of speeches *Arguments for Socialism*: 'The whole purpose of the planning agreement is to introduce that democratic tripartite element into industrial policy. That is the unique contribution that the shop floor and labour movement made in the development of policy.' So here at Vickers we had a microcosm of this 'unique contribution'. Not under ideal conditions I agree - the original industrial policies had been considerably weakened - but you did have a left-wing minister, Les Huckfield, in charge of the Vickers case. He was involved in these tripartite discussions. What happened, what was the result? Vickers made a few promises just as would any tactically astute company within a planning agreement. The workers, encouraged by these promises went back to Tyneside, lifted their industrial sanctions - probably the one thing that led to the tripartite meeting anyway. Two weeks later, Vickers (strengthened by the announcement of the general election) forgot its promises and confirmed the decision to close. The Labour government stood by and the workers, demoralised and defeated, took the redundancy money and joined the dole queues of Tyneside - by which time Stuart Holland was MP for Vauxhall.

Applause

That's not a cheap point! But in a sense the final outcome - Stuart an MP and the workers defeated - symbolises the conflict between the two views of political power which the experience as a whole illustrates. Of course I am not blaming Stuart Holland for the closure. The Vickers management and the Labour government must bear the main responsibility; and there were weaknesses in the shop floor leadership. I am showing that the belief in the government's ability to really control big companies has the effect, often unintended, of substituting for and diverting from building the direct political power of the workers' own organisations. And that is in spite of what the Labour left would say. Because of course Stuart would have liked nothing more than a strike in support of a planning agreement - industrial action in support of the government intervening. But you can't turn workers' political action on and off like a tap. If you advise them that parliament has the power to control Vickers, if you're elected to parliament on the basis that parliament has got the power to control the big corporations, then the workers' organisations whose pressure the Labour left find they need are not prepared; they haven't thought of themselves as having political power. They might lobby, they might demonstrate, but that's not what we're talking about. Political power means the power to control and that means workers' and community organisations, the extra-parliamentary organisations, seeing *themselves* as political organisations. But if your prime focus is on the power of parliament, if that's the basis of your involvement with extra-parliamentary organisations, then in a sense you hold back and deflect and substitute for the new ways of organising and the self-confidence necessary for these organisations to exert political power. Because to develop themselves as political organisations requires a fantastic break from traditional ways of organising. It requires a break from the traditional division between politics and industry, between political action and trade union action, on which the Labour Party and the trade unions are based. It requires new links between shop stewards committees across companies, across industries and public services; between them and community based organisations. In a way the defeat of Tony Benn's policies in the last Labour government and the fact that there was no counter pressure from shop stewards to support and back them up further illustrates this incompatibility between the Labour left's policies and the difficult requirements of extra-parliamentary strength and action. In the build-up to those industrial policies there was no lack of a good relationship between Tony Benn and shop stewards - they worshipped the ground he trod on. In a sense that was the problem. For it shows how the nature of the relationship was built up on the idea of what Labour ministers, using parliament, could achieve for workers outside. So when those policies were defeated the shop stewards committees themselves took no action, there was no pressure because they themselves had not been prepared to act politically; that had been left, the assumption being that it was parliament's job to exert control over corporations.

I think also the success of the anti-Corrie Bill campaign is an illustration of this point in reverse because the anti-Corrie campaign was no ordinary sort of lobbying back-up to MPs. It was successful because of the powerful political movement that had been built by women over the last ten years, not just outside parliament, but for whose struggles parliament was completely marginal. In this way even a defensive parliamentary victory depended on the strength of a movement whose growth has been based on the realisation that parliament had failed to achieve even the most basic ideals of a democratic society.

So far I've been talking about the power to achieve socialism but the other side of the Labour left's reliance on a power which is illusory, the power of parliament, is that socialism has less and less credibility and attraction to the majority of working-class people. This is the main feature of the crisis facing the left. In most people's mind socialism has always been associated with the extending of state control over the economy to achieve full employment, to build and maintain the welfare state. Now that the particular economic conditions for that have collapsed parliament has seemed impotent and, in the face of pressures from private capital and the IMF, it no longer seems a credible means of popular control. As a result the state is experienced as an alien, often a hostile institution. The socialism associated with the state and trying to reform it therefore loses its attraction: I think this partly explains why, in what used to be the strongholds of statist socialism - places like Tyneside, South Wales, and Merseyside - there is such demoralisation and such a pervasive sense of there being no alternative to fight for.

But against this background of the weakening of socialism in those traditional strongholds, areas where statist socialism had been strongest, there are movements which have grown, initiatives which have captured people's imagination on a wide scale. They express a different image of socialism, based on self-organisation: like the women's movement, the Anti-Nazi League and Rock Against Racism and the sort of anti-authoritarian, anti-state culture which has been generated among the young people. Other examples are the initiative of the Lucas workers to produce a plan for socially useful production, and the occupations of hospitals which go beyond defensive action against the cuts and raise the issues of control and the kind of health service we want. Then there are the numerous attempts to create a culture of resistance through local working class publishing projects, socialist theatre groups, bookshops, socialist centres and clubs. All those initiatives have been based on asserting the power of people organising at a shop floor and community level without any *reliance* on the parliament, though support is gratefully received. The other thing about them which points to the future of the left, is that they're not just extra-parliamentary, not just militant but (although the initial impetus has been defensive) in the ways they've organised, in the culture they've created, in the relationships they've developed with each other, they've provided an image and an alternative of the society we want to create and have therefore created something worth fighting for.

We haven't yet found a way of organising that can consolidate some of the gains of these growth points and extend and generalise their insights. But clearly the whole idea of them being organised through the Labour Party, a Party whose whole rationale is winning parliamentary power, would drain the very life blood from those movements.

I fear also that the revolutionary organisations, when they put the building of their own parties before everything else, similarly drain and frustrate the political confidence and political growth of those movements.

So what we have to do is find a way of organising, find a way of developing socialist politics through which we're neither the vanguards nor the supporting spectators of these movements but through which we act as catalysts, deeply involved in extending the political power and developing the political coherence of these movements. There's an obvious urgency about this, an urgency in both rejecting a primarily parliamentary sort of politics, and on the other hand ridding the revolutionary organisations of the sectarianism they still contain; because it is only the power of the extra-parliamentary movements which could lead to the overthrow of the Tories; it is only the political coherence of the alternatives they develop which is going to make for more than just another Tory Labour government, whether led by Healey or by someone from the Labour left.

Applause

Peter Hain

Now Paul Foot from Socialist Workers' Party. Before Paul opens up can I just remind those who want to make contributions from the floor that they'll have to be two minute contributions, can you hand speaker's slips to the stewards putting your name and your organisation on them.

PAUL FOOT

Comrades I find it very difficult to follow Stuart's rather interesting account of Gramsci in the thirties, because I find myself preoccupied by the problems which beset us now. We have a Tory government rampaging through the country, slashing and stabbing whatever they can as though they were an invading army and we have a rotten opposition to it. I'm worried about the opposition to it. Look at the places that people look to for opposition to the Tory government; it's not coming from there. Whenever you see a Labour minister in Parliament attacking the Tory government they get the same reply; the reply is: 'You did it too'.

Applause

Now then, I was reading a debate the other day on the National Health Service charges in the House of Commons - Stanley Orme the representative for the Labour Party on this matter, was challenging the Tories on the prescription charges for health. He makes all the arguments about the prescription charges, explains that we don't want to penalise the sick, we don't want any charges at all for drugs, spectacles, teeth or anything of that kind - when up jumps Patrick Jenkin.

Who is Patrick Jenkin? He's the Secretary of State for Social Security and Health. The reason that he's Minister of Health is that he was for a long time legal adviser to the Distillers' company during the time that they were making Thalidomide! But he knows how to put the Labour spokesman on the spot, and he said 'Doesn't Stanley realise that the first government to introduce prescription charges on health was a Labour government? Doesn't he know that every subsequent Labour government imposed prescription charges on health right throughout the field?' And Stanley got up to reply - I have his reply here - he said 'I admit that the introduction of charges by a Labour government was regrettable.'

Now every time that any subject is raised the same reply comes. Take the question of unemployment. The Tories say 'You're worried about unemployment. You doubled it. We haven't doubled it. We're trying to, we're doing our best to double it, but we haven't doubled it yet. Are you worried about the cuts? Your cuts in 1976 were worse in percentage terms than our cuts are today. Are you worried about prices? You doubled them. We haven't doubled them yet. Doing our best, going along the same roads, you opened the door, we're coming in, what are you complaining about?'

Everywhere you look the parliamentary opposition is frustrated by these replies and the industrial opposition is frustrated too. The industrial opposition - much more serious in a way - that we'd watched when the trade union movement responded in the seventies so clearly to the way in which the Tories were carrying on. The trade union movement at Leyland, in the South Wales pits, in the steel strike obeying calls to the bosses' ballots, splitting the very solidarity which helped to hit the Tories before - we can see that being split. Why? Because for five years under a Labour government they were treated by their leaders as a stage army, told they couldn't go for more than the particular amount of money that was laid down by trade union leaders operating with the Labour government. And the stage armies, when called upon to fight for the very basic liberties that keep the whole trade union movement together, the stage armies aren't prepared to come out any longer.

Why was the Labour government so awful? That's the question we have to ask. Why did it behave in the way in which it did and here's one reply. One reply right away: Because they were not in charge, not in charge of what they were doing. Here's another example: An example on the question of gas prices, a very topical matter, raised in parliament on 28 March 1977. A Labour back bencher: 'Why is the Labour government forcing up gas prices? Isn't that an insult to all the trade unionists that made all these sacrifices over the years?' The question was answered by the Secretary of State for Energy at that time whose name for the moment escapes me: 'I think that any increase in prices is' - Oh, here we are again - 'regrettable, but my honourable friend will know that this increase arrived from the necessity to reduce the public sector borrowing requirement in connection with the IMF loan.' You see Tony Benn didn't make the decisions, he just announced them. You go around and you see people with badges nowadays saying 'Don't blame me, I voted Labour'. I think Tony should get one made for himself which says: 'Don't blame me, I was just the Secretary of State, I didn't do the things responsible!' It wasn't just the IMF, (and IMF doesn't stand for the Institute of Workers' Control, the IMF stands for the International Monetary Fund - groups of bankers not elected by anyone). This is from The Confessions of Tony Benn, *Arguments for Socialism*, a book that came out recently: 'I discovered' - this is his experience in government - 'I discovered' - a sort of Saul of Tarsus operation - 'how the immense power of the bankers and the industrialists in Britain and worldwide could be used to bring direct and indirect pressure again backed by the media first to halt and then to reverse the policy of a Labour government that both the electors and the House of Commons have accepted.'

The power of bankers, industrialists - let's add to it, judges, civil servants, police chiefs, army chiefs - all these sort of people who are not elected but are bound together by the solidarity of property with no election to back them up, are able - we hear from somebody who was there at the time, you don't have to hear from us on the outside but somebody on the inside - able to *halt* and *reverse* the policies of the Labour government. Where does that leave us now? It leaves us quite clearly in the circumstances in which it is quite ridiculous to start providing new programmes. New programmes! Who knows that these programmes will be carried out! No point in thinking about appointing new trade union leaders, a new set of leaders with a new set of policies when the rank and file don't even follow the trade union leaders on ordinary elementary trade union liberties questions.

And therefore the question comes out clear. It screams from all this experience of the last five years, screams at us, that it is the foundations of the movement that are rotting and it's no good, when the foundations of the movement are rotting, mucking about with the superstructure. We've got to go back to where the power is, not where it isn't, not in parliament, not in trade union offices but where it is - on the shop floor, in the rank and file ...

Applause

... And we need socialist agitation at the rank and file more than we ever did before, because in the fifties and sixties militancy was enough, it was enough to say that we must be militant to gain more from a boss. Now that isn't enough. Now if you ask why, *why* was the decision taken in the South Wales pits, *why*, the answer is that there is a fear in the movement now, a fear of the whole prop of existence, the job, the whole security of existence being knocked out from under you and the argument that comes and is so cleverly used in all the Tory media is - 'what's the point in making steel when nobody buys steel, what's the point in that?' There's only one reply to it - the reply being: 'why is there a steel recession in the first place, why is nobody buying steel? Is it because nobody needs steel; is it because the whole of India, South East Asia, Africa is so stuffed with steel products that they don't need any more? Is that the explanation? Is there a glut in steel all over the world? Is that the explanation?' No, obviously it's not the explanation. Running side by side you have on the one hand the tremendous capacity to produce, the capacity to feed the world not once but twice over, the capacity to provide everything that people need and yes, everything that they want, that's there, available to us now. But on the other hand there is this increasing poverty and desperation all the time matching the ability to produce and the increasing poverty running side by side. Why? Because the society is divided up, controlled by people only interested in their property and their privileges and splitting the society and exploiting the society and stumbling from boom to slump. The socialist argument is only powerful in the rank and file where it can give force and power to the people who've got the power to change the society - that's where we have to do the agitation and that's where we have to do the organising.

Now I believe that what I've said up to now is, generally speaking, agreed. I think that really what I've said is probably agreed by Tony Benn, probably even by Stuart Holland, although I found it so difficult to follow what he was saying. But I think probably they agreed with what I'm saying, yes, we do need to go back, we do need to go back to the rank and file, we do need to operate there in the rank and file. But what they are saying - which is clear from what Stuart said right at the end when he called upon us to join the Labour Party - what the argument is, and it's a very powerful and attractive argument, the argument goes like this: 'Yes we need rank and file agitation, we need more socialists in the rank and file, we need more extra-parliamentary activity of the type which converted Tony Benn at the Upper Clyde Shipbuilding sit-in in 1971. We need more of that today and we need to forge it into a powerful Labour Party which will go alongside radical socialist politics and which will protect the next Labour government against the ravages of bankers, industrialists judges and all the rest of them.'

Now that's what the argument is and it's a very attractive one and I reply to it like this. That we see the two traditions of activity, the extra-parliamentary rank and file organisation if you like on the one hand, and the parliamentary organisation on the other. We see them as two different roads running in different directions. Running very often, when it comes to the end (though in a debate like this they seem to run together), but when it comes to the crunch again and again running into one another. This is something that you can't fudge, that you have to choose between them - a lot of the things that Hilary said pointed that contradiction out - and to demonstrate what I mean I want to talk a little bit about the Labour Party itself. You see, it's true that when Labour had to win the workers' vote, when it had to win the vote from the Tories and from the Liberals, to win people's minds away from all that old obsequiousness to the boss which they had then and their obsession with the Liberal Party - to do all those things they required agitation - mass agitation.

One of the first jobs I did was to be a reporter in the by-election at Bridgetown in the East End of Glasgow in 1961. I read up the history of that period, I read about the history of when they first elected an ILP candidate in Bridgetown in 1922. In that area of Glasgow then, the whole place ran with agitation. In every close mouth there was an ILP representative, in every street an ILP bulletin and that was reflected all over the country. All the way through the period of winning the vote for Labour through the twenties, thirties, forties yes, right up until 1950. There were newspapers for instance, national newspapers with massive circulation. The *Daily Herald* for most of it's life was owned or controlled by the Labour Party or the TUC. The Cooperative Party, which was part of the Labour Party, owned or controlled the *News* which was read by hundreds of thousands of workers on Sundays, and there were libraries created, all the way through Britain especially South Wales, massive working-class libraries, books lovingly collected out of the pennies of workers in which people were taught to read about their own literature, literature that came out of their class, not the crap that they got in school or on the radio. And there's a whole history there of agitation in order to win the vote.

But the point about this history of agitation is that all of it was linked to the parliamentary process, all of it was linked to the business of winning the vote and it followed then as night followed day that as soon as the vote was won, as soon as it became clear that millions of people, almost by automatic reaction, were going to vote Labour, then the agitation collapsed and since 1951 or 1952 you have an absolutely irretrievable pattern of the collapse of agitation, and the collapse of involvement in the Labour Party. The newspapers that I've mentioned were either sold or closed. The libraries have all been sold off to dealers. The whole business of local activity and local discussion has collapsed. Individual membership in the Labour Party has declined by something quite extraordinary and all of it is a process that is inevitable because the thing was attached only to that little slender little bit of democracy which was voting MPs into Parliament.

Then there was another process and we've seen a bit of that process here today, that every time a Labour government faltered or every time it was beaten you had another process of agitation coming into the fore. You had the Labour left in one form or another coming and saying: 'Now comrades we've lost or we've faltered. Now we need a bit of agitation. Come on out all you extra-parliamentarians, let's debate with you in the Central Hall, let's have a discussion, let's get you working again because that's the only way we'll ever get into office again. Come on let's get moving.' They may mean it sincerely. Let's bind it together as I've described earlier. This goes way way back. In 1925, the Lansbury Clubs; in the 1930s the Socialist League - Stafford Cripps and Aneurin Bevan; in the 1940s, the Keep Left Group organised by that well known revolutionary and fellow columnist of mine on *Daily Mirror* newspapers, Woodrow Wyatt; in the 1950s, Victory for Socialism; in the 1960s, Appeal for Unity - all different attempts in opposition or when the government was faltering to bring together extra-parliamentary agitation; to try and raise again socialist consciousness in the rank and file, to try and lift what Shelley called the 'spirit that lifts the slave before his Lord', trying to do that again through the Labour Party and in the Labour Party. But because that was where they operated, first of all each group was weaker than the last - the Labour Coordinating Committee is at the end of this line - I don't mean in terms of winning votes on the Labour Party National Executive but weaker in mass terms; and the other thing about it is that as it got weaker so it was less and less able to have any effect. And, secondly, on each occasion the agitation was neatly packed away in time for an election, and everyone was called on to make 'a united heave' to get Labour back into office. All this was quite logical. Why? Because it was all happening apart from the things that are going on in the outside world, always going on separate to all the activities and struggles that are happening in the strikes, the agitation and all the things that I was talking about earlier, those things are separately, yes, separate to how the Labour Party conducts its agitation and that's why we say, we say that the Labour Party process is linked inextricably to the passivity of the masses, that the masses have to be passive in those circumstances and all the people who join the Labour Party as agitators to change the world, all of them become not changers of the world but changed themselves in the process. Lansbury, Cripps, Nye Bevan, Wyatt, Sidney Silverman, Lord Greenwood, Peter Hain - where is he going to be - will he join this list or will he help us build an alternative?

That's the question that we want to put tonight. What I'm saying is this. What is the alternative?

Let me talk a little about the alternative. And how I see the alternative. First of all what Hilary was saying about for whom is this alternative. For people who see that because of the way in which the society is constituted, equality, a socialist society is not going to be won just by 'decent' processes; that those people who have property will not surrender that property, they will not surrender it even in events where parliamentary legislation threatens their power. If parliamentary legislation threatens their property then, and we have the example of Chile staring at us down the barrel of a gun, they will shoot the opposition rather than give power to it. That's the first thing. The second question is this, just what Hilary was saying. What sort of socialism are we interested in? What is the socialism that we're interested in? Is it, as she put it, just a question of more state control, dictatorial, tyrannical, what about Russia, is it like the sort of society that we have in Czechoslovakia and Russia today? And I believe that if you say to people 'look, we'll do it for you, you keep quiet and we'll do the job for you' then the suspicion, the suspicion that exists in people's minds that socialism is something dictated from above, the suspicion increases, it becomes more rigid. Now if you say we have to get it from below, we have to organise from below that there's more socialism in a strike committee at Stocksbridge working out the hardship fund, there's more of socialism there than in all the plans of the Labour Party, then you begin to see a new and different form of organisation, an organisation which is tied to people's activities.

First of all, the important units are not geographical, the important units are industrial, where people spend most of their active lives - the industrial unit being the important one where people spend most of their working lives, where they co-operate most together, where they contribute most together and where, because they produce there, they have the power. The important units of organisation being there and the activity of the organisation corresponding to the aspirations of where people are fighting, where they are fighting, where they are battling. It is not just a question of where they're on strike but where they're fighting, all the thousands of little agitations that take place over, I don't know, housing, the no-disconnections campaign, yes, the Irish campaign to get the troops out of Ireland, to free the Irish political prisoners, all those hundreds of agitations that go on day by day. The Party has to be organised around those agitations, organised around them so that it's able to correspond there, so that it's able to say 'yes, we put our socialist influence here, there, where there are people fighting'. We use our socialist effort to initiate other struggles and we're constantly on the look out for where the real battle is - not in parliament, not in trade union offices but where people are beginning to fight.

That's really a form of organisation which is not something that is a corollary to parliamentary organisation but something which constantly runs against it, constantly clashes with it. You constantly find the parliamentarians trying to put down that organisation, that's the history of our movement. There are always such clashes, you have to realise that. Rosa Luxemburg was shot not by a Tory government but by a Labour government and by the orders of a Labour government. What happened in Portugal in 1974? The great bursting, enthusiasm of workers in Portugal in 1974 was held back and sucked dry by this parliamentary process and we say therefore that there are two different traditions, two different traditions, two different forms of organisation.

I believe that what we've done in the Socialist Workers' Party is why we're here tonight. We have tried to build an organisation like that, over the last ten, perhaps twenty years we've tried to build it. Peter said: 'We're weaker now than we were ten years ago.' That's not my experience. Ten years ago the SWP hardly existed. We're much more effective now than we were ten years ago and in the interim we have done a lot of things, tiny though the organisation is, we have done a lot of things. For instance to mobilise the unemployed, for instance to build the united activity against the Nazis which Peter was talking about earlier. We've also established a presence in a number of areas of the working class where there is a socialist confidence and a socialist conviction. And the point is this: that if it were the case that we had not twenty dockers, but one hundred and twenty, then I believe that the impact of the steel blockade - the thing that Moss Evans discovered after nine weeks of the steel strike - would have been much more powerful. I believe that if we'd had a few more of those members it would have been more powerful there. If we'd had more engineers and more people in Leyland, not six in Leyland but sixty or even six hundred, then the circumstances in Leyland would have been different. In other words I can see out of this form of activity some sort of hope for change, change now, not just change for the future, change now, immediate reforms, people living a better life - and hope for the future that the transformation of society into an egalitarian democracy is possible from the bottom up. I can see some hope in these circumstances. I don't believe that the Labour left can see any hope in that at all.

Now what I do when I speak up and down the country is end up by calling on people to join the Socialist Workers' Party and I mean that.

Applause

I do that again tonight. But I don't want to end there. I don't want to end just by calling on people to join the Socialist Workers' Party because I like the spirit in which this meeting has been called. I think it's been called in a fraternal spirit and a spirit which really is worried, as we're worried, as everyone else is worried, about the state of opposition to the Tories and what happens in the future. I also recognise, and it would be stupid for anyone not to recognise, that we in the Socialist Workers' Party and more so the other organisations in my view are still haunted by the spectre of sectarianism that hangs over us ...

Applause

... hangs over us, this awful bigoted, certainty and arrogance that we have all the answers conducted in a sort of language which other people don't understand. Now we've been trying for years and years to get away from that, and we're still trying, and we are interested in coming together with other people in the fight against the Tories. But we're interested in coming together not in words, not even just in debates, but in activity. We're interested in united activity, united activity against the union bill, against the cuts, yes, united activity to get those troops out of Ireland and those political prisoners out of the prisons there.

Applause

If each of you tonight were to think where it is that they could do something to change the world we live in and to roll back the priorities of the Tory government and no doubt of the next Labour government, no doubt of the next Labour government, then I believe the meeting will have achieved something and I believe that if you do do those things then I'm quite confident that we will win the argument in the end in that activity. But what I implore you is: Don't take refuge from the Tories in what they call the 'broad church' of the Labour Party. Broad it may be. It wasn't broad when I was in it! But church it certainly is. You can go back in there and Tony will read you a lesson - what is it Tony, from the prophet Micah? - and there will be people there in strange silent ways passing strange silent resolutions behind slow whispering doors. But you can be absolutely sure that those things happen in spite of and ignoring the very bitter battles that are going to take place outside. Don't go back in there comrades because one more time of a Labour government elected with even more radical promises than the last one, but able to deliver even less, will land us all in troubles that none of us have even imagined. I'll leave you with a quotation from the famous black freedom fighter, Frederick Douglas, in America. When they told him: 'Fred, come on we've found a new way of winning freedom for the black people - we can go into the nice educated houses of nice educated Americans and they will win nice educated freedom for the blacks by nice educated legislation', Frederick Douglas had a very, very simple answer to that: 'Without struggle there is no progress, and those who profess to favour freedom yet deprecate agitation - Why? They want the crops without digging up the ground; they want the ocean without the awful roar of its waters.'

Applause

Peter Hain

I realise that there are some would-be football referees in the audience but I hope that you will allow the debate to continue. Tony Benn!

TONY BENN

Comrades I think it would be a sad thing, when the media prevents us speaking to each other every day, if on the one occasion when we do get together we shout so loud we can't even hear each other in this hall.

Lot of heckling here and sound of whistle blowing.

If we are ready to continue and the issue is about Ireland I'll tell you my view, and it's always been my view. I was brought up to believe that the partition of Ireland was a crime against the Irish people, I've said so on many occasions and I ...

Applause

... recently proposed to the National Executive Committee that the unity and independence of Ireland should be set as an objective in the terms of reference of our new committee on Irish policy to be reached by consent. But having said that I must also tell you that I do not believe that the immediate withdrawal of the troops from Ireland would be a solution to that problem.

My starting point is a very simple one. It is that everybody here who call themselves socialists are part of the failure that we are discussing. I say that without criticism of others. But in fairness Paul Foot has had the absolute freedom to organise the SWP for many years and go round and make his impassioned speeches. He is part of the failure just as I am who has served in Labour governments since 1964. I go further than that and I give you two examples.

First, the idea that it's all right at the grass roots. In this hall about a month ago I spoke at a demonstration against the Corrie Bill and I said to the meeting, mainly made up of women, that it was right that we should support the campaign against the Corrie Bill and that the women should support the steel workers. There was violent opposition to that statement from some of the crowd who shouted: 'It's nothing to do with us about the steel workers.' Then last night I was speaking at a steel strike committee in South Wales and when we were talking about the media one of the steel workers said 'And when we have a Labour paper, let's have a nude on page 2 and page 3 in order to boost the circulation' without realising what he'd said, and not meaning it. But one reason why some women voted the Thatcher government into power which is now cutting back on the steel industry was that they suspected the trade unions did not back women's rights. Therefore what we have to do is to recognise that we may be an enthusiastic audience of socialists but we do not have a majority of support outside for any of our solutions to the problems: neither the solution of the socialist groups, nor the solution that is put forward by the Labour Party.

This is not an academic debate, at least that's not how I see it, it is not a test of socialist credentials and I have brought no quotations from Paul Foot or Tariq Ali.

Applause

I see no winners and I see no losers amongst us. The starting point must be what is happening now, how did we get here, and how do socialists respond in a way that is successful. First how do we defend the interests of those we try to represent? Secondly how do we enlarge the political consciousness of our own people? How do we campaign for change? Hilary Wainwright, in my opinion, put the most important question of all which is: how do you inter-relate the efforts of people at the place of work to the work of the trade unions and the political parties at national level, and above all, when you've got a support how do you carry it through?

To have had a discussion without any reference to the fact that Britain is caught in a world slump with a weakened capitalist system and with deliberate policy of de-industrialisation would be to leave out the background against which we meet and to miss the major problem that we have now to discuss. The fact is that we have a capitalist system in this country which is no longer capable of sustaining the welfare upon which so much of our post-war politics rested. The real problem is not that the Tory government are pursuing their policy, but that there is no alternative to their policy unless we are prepared to achieve 'a fundamental and irreversible shift in the balance of wealth and power in favour of working people and their families', if I may be allowed to quote myself for I am myself responsible for setting that objective for the labour movement in 1973. The last Labour government, within the framework of market forces, did try to protect the people it sought to represent. It is no good pretending that there is no difference between the Thatcher policy and the policy of successive Labour governments because if you do that you destroy the credibility upon which support must rest. The Labour government did, in some respects, shift the balance of power by the repeal of the Industrial Relations Act and by erecting the Health and Safety Act and the Employment Protection Act. The reality is that we have come as far as can possibly be advanced within the basically capitalist system. Indeed we have come now to the point where the capitalist system cannot even allow us to sustain the gains that were made before. It is true that socialists, both inside and outside the Labour Party, have said all this before. It is the role of socialists to look ahead, and our privilege to be proved right. But I would say this to colleagues who are not members of the Labour Party. To forecast the future correctly is not the same as to forecast the remedies that would succeed in changing that future. That is the great difficulty that we confront. If the Labour Party has not achieved socialism neither have the socialist groups. It would be a great mistake if we were to pretend at this meeting that this is just a matter of allocating blame and then going home again and starting all over again.

I am not here to ask for your support for me. What I am saying is that the Labour Party has made formidable gains since 1945 in the maintenance of full employment, the development of the welfare state, the extension of public ownership and the establishment of trade union rights. I accept that much of this was the unfinished business of the 1906 Liberal government but it laid the foundations for welfare capitalism which had a profound effect upon a significant section of the

Labour Party in diverting them from socialism. I don't say the whole Labour Party gave up socialism. This was one of Paul Foot's errors. He detected no difference in his analysis between some sections of the Labour Party, the Parliamentary Party and trade union leadership, and the socialist case that has been consistently argued by the Labour Conference. But it is true that, from 1959 and basing themselves on the apparent success of welfare capitalism, there was an attack upon socialism within the Labour Party reflected by the attempt to repeal Clause 4, the breach with the unions, and the attack on the role of Conference. There was also the abandonment of self-government in two important contexts: one, the decision of a small majority of a Labour cabinet to recommend our membership of the Common Market, and second, the acceptance of American missiles in the United Kingdom without a British veto.

Having said all that I must repeat that a Labour government was better than Thatcher then and it would be better than Thatcher now. But the policies it followed would not be good enough to tackle the problems that have now to be tackled.

I emphasise better than Thatcher then and now because the problem that Paul Foot and Hilary Wainwright speak about - 'why doesn't the agitation continue when Labour is in power?' - is because the rank and file of the Labour Party know that it is better to have a Labour government than a Tory government and they are not prepared to put it at risk. Paul thinks that it is parliamentarians who go and persuade the rank and file to stop agitation. The reality is that the rank and file of the labour movement do not want to put at risk the survivial of a Labour government. We must be prepared to face the fact that the problem of the balance between agitation and loyalty has got to be solved. Unless we can deal with that problem we are going to continue to be radical in opposition and somewhat conservative in power.

Comrades there must be so many people from MI5, people from the MI6, the CIA and the KGB here that I'm not sure they aren't the ones who are shouting! Please be very careful that we don't prevent ourselves from having a serious discussion. Let me say this about Ireland. Nobody could argue that when a Labour government was in power the agitation for Irish independence and unity didn't continue. It did, but even that was not successful in achieving a real debate in this country about policy in Ireland without which we shall not solve the problem. I genuinely plead to those who come to this meeting to put the Irish issue on the agenda, not to organise themselves in such a way as to prevent this discussion or anything else from taking place.

If we are serious we have got also to ask why it is that the socialist groups have also failed to prove the efficacy of their own solution. I think the reason lies in an analysis that we must go through. First of all most of the socialist groups have confused the absence of reform with the failure of reform. The real complaint that I have is not that we reformed and it failed, but that we didn't reform. That is what the argument going on within the Labour Party at the moment is all about. It is that industry was not reformed, despite the 1973 programme. It is that the banks were not reformed despite the policy of Conference. Parliament was not reformed despite the insistent demand for the abolition for the House of Lords. The media were not reformed despite the reports made by the Party and put before Conference. The civil service was not reformed. Education was not reformed. The control of the police and the security services was not reformed.

I say to this meeting, if you'll listen to me, that reform is an honourable and radical course. To argue that what is wrong is that the reforms have failed is to miss the reality. They have not been carried through.

I believe there is a very important relationship here between what Hilary Wainwright said and what I am saying. I have had many shop stewards come to see me from UCS onwards to raise their problems with the minister. What they did not want from a Labour minister was a lecture on the efficacy of revolutionary socialism. What they wanted was a solution to their problem now, and the opportunity to learn from their experience as to how to safeguard jobs and change society on a wider scale. But if anybody really imagines that when a group of shop stewards, from Alfred Herbert or from British Leyland or from Ferranti or from UCS or from the River Don Steel Works, had been treated to an address on revolutionary socialism by a Labour minister, that they would have been more likely to respond to that government, they are totally misunderstanding what it is about. If we only talk to those who have major problems about revolution then they will say to us: 'You are trying to use *our* crisis to promote *your* revolution. We want to use *you*, the Labour movement and the Labour leadership to solve *our* problems.'

I warn those who think that agitation - important as it is to clarify issues - is the same as preaching revolution to those who come to a Labour government to settle their problems, that they really do miss the point. Of course we must go on to learn the lessons that go beyond individual cases. The Labour Party is a reforming socialist party and that is the basis upon which it operates.

Now I come to the second criticism: and that is that the socialist groups confuse real reform with revolution. They want reform and talk of revolution. It implies, and nobody believes it, that there is a short cut to the transfer of power in this country. It implies that a violent overthrow with power passing to others would, by some coup d'etat by vanguard forces, without consent, create a democratic socialist system that would, in some way erode the power of the state. Most people know that to do it that way revolutionary groups would have to seize the power of the state and use it against those who disagree. It ignores all the historical evidence. Stalin had no more choice in my judgement, than Mrs Thatcher has given the fact that she has inherited a collapsing capitalism and he had inherited a post-revolutionary communist state. I believe that the socialist groups are not serious revolutionaries at all. What the socialist groups in this country really do is to analyse, to think, to support struggle, to criticise the Labour Party, to expand consciousness, to preach a better morality. These are all very desirable things to do. But they have very little to do with revolution. In effect they help to create a demand for real reform.

The third error of the groups is that they misread the role of democracy in parliament as one instrument for real reform. The reason the labour movement will never give up its belief in parliamentary democracy is that it rightly believes it created parliamentary democracy. That is why it will never give up its support for it. Whatever may be said by the modern theorists of the socialist groups, the Chartist campaigns and the suffragette campaigns cannot be dismissed as having lead to a fraudulent advance. It was a real advance. And anyone who thinks the labour movement ever gave up extra-parliamentary struggle in favour of parliamentary reform must have been asleep over the last thirty years. What do you think happened in 1974 when the miners struck and created circumstances in which the government went to the country? How do you think we won our liberties except by struggle? How do you imagine that the Corrie Bill was beaten except by a combination of the efforts of the women's movement with the efforts of those in parliament?

The difficulty that the socialist groups are in, and I think they must face it, is that they are confusing extra-parliamentary struggle, which I fully support, with anti-parliamentary campaigning which invites the labour movement to repudiate its past. It is absolutely absurd to invite the labour movement to abandon its concept of the role of parliamentary change as a part of its great campaigns. Here is the paradox: What is the ballot box but a revolution? Of course it is a revolution. I invite you to go round the world today, and find how many people would give up their lives for the right to do what we can do which is to dismiss our government when it comes to a general election. I think that Paul Foot's party and the IMG and the other socialist groups are so small partly because people fear that if power was acquired the way Paul and Tariq and the other groups wish to acquire it, the people would lose the right to dismiss them if they were not satisfied with what followed.

My next point is that in saying that the labour movement has failed, Paul Foot preaches defeatism. He argues that it has not only failed but it must always fail and he cites Allende. Well on that definition let me give him some other 'failures' of history: Tolpuddle was a failure, Lansbury was a failure, Clay Cross was a failure, Grunwick was a failure, Rosa Luxemburg was a failure, Trotsky was a failure - because the people involved did not achieve in their lifetime the objectives which they set themselves. Yet we all know that in reality none of these were failures. Our only strength lies in our unity and our confidence. Those who preach defeatism are not revolutionaries. They are left-talking revolutionists, who are trying to destroy the two pillars of our strength which are, our unity and our belief that if we organise within the labour movement we can change society.

What then comrades should we do now? I believe that we must build upon our historical strength and I believe that there is a great deal more than we have recognised in the moral values of socialism against the rotten values of capitalism. We must support the women's movements, the blacks, the environmentalists, the peace movements and those who are trying to bring about a peaceful united Ireland. We must build the unions, we must put forward a socialist analysis, we must have democracy in the Labour Party.

The Labour Party is a socialist party. But what it does believe and I think it is right, is this: that if you rely upon an ideological scholasticism alone to guide you, you will splinter as the SWP expelled the Revolutionary Communist Group and they expelled the Revolutionary Communist Tendency, and the Revolutionary Communist Tendency has now given birth to the The Discussion Group. The splintering and disintegration of the left - very evident at this meeting - is, in the view of the Labour Party, a source of weakness. We believe that experience will educate us in socialism, and unite us. What Hilary said about the women's movement is very important. What may begin as a non-political movement saying 'it's only about women's rights' will progress when people begin to ask themselves whether that is really true. If half the places in the grammar schools were taken by women is that the equality the feminist movement wants? Not at all. If half the chairmen of the multinational corporations were women, is that the achievement that would be wanted? No. I believe there is a very important place for socialist groups discussing and working on the problems of society. There are many of them. We have not got on this platform the Communist Party, the New Communist Party, the Socialist Party of Great Britain, the Marxist-Leninists. We have not got the Revolutionary Communist Group or the Revolutionary Communist Tendency. We have not got the Spartacists or the Posadists, the Workers' Revolutionary Party or the Workers Socialist League.

There is no substitute for united action within a united Labour Party. How can we improve the prospects. By amalgamation? No. By popular front? No. By collective entryism to expose, polarise and split the Labour Party? No. By taking each issue, by cooperation on racialism, on the women's movement, on peace, on jobs - Yes, as the Anti-Nazi League has shown and by individuals who want to contribute joining the Labour Party. We must also retain the centres of socialist thought represented by the various journals that are published. I do not imagine that the leaders of these groups will want to join the Labour Party as it would be impertinent to suggest that they do. But I do invite those who are members of no groups, or those who have served in one, or other, or many of the splinter groups, to consider what is happening in the Labour Party today.

The radicalisation of the main body of the labour movement, the genuine restatement of the socialist case, the debate on democracy in the Labour Party today is sharper and more real than it has ever been. That is the case for democratic socialism. I can only lay one claim for it, and that is that the British Labour Party is the instrument of the British working class movement and nobody here can deny it whatever view they may take. What we offer is unity of action plus diversity of thought - a pluralism within a democratic movement.

I may say this in conclusion. If the Labour Party fails it does not follow that there will be a swing to the socialist groups. My own opinion is that if the Labour Party and the Socialist groups in Britain attack each other, as happened in Germany before the war, you could easily move into a fascist situation in Britain. And it does not follow that socialism will emerge automatically phoenix-like from the ashes of fascism. We've had the experience of Italy and Germany, Spain and Portugal. When fascism was destroyed it did not follow that democratic socialism automatically emerged.

The British working-class movement created the British Labour Party and we have the means to win consent for socialism by democracy. Any other sort of socialism is unachievable and would not be worth having even if it could be achieved. That is my case.

Applause

Peter Hain

And now for contributions from the floor. Speakers will be asked to speak for two minutes; after one minute you'll get a buzz and after two minutes we're going to have to stop you on the red light. I want to call Steve Hart first and after him Paul Acaster.

STEVE HART

We are in a crisis not only in terms of the economy, the de-industrialisation of Britain, but also we are facing an acute crisis on the left. Because we are in a situation in which after many years of right-wing social democratic government there is not the kind of popular socialist consciousness that there was in the past. The main point I want to make here is that I think it's a grave mistake that there is not a Communist Party speaker on the platform because I think the Communist Party is the largest marxist organisation on the left, the longest established, and has profound roots in the working class. And that is very important as speakers have mentioned. I think what's more, the *British Road to Socialism* is the most advanced strategic response to the crisis in terms of the central problem of the left and the relationship of politics to the working class, in dealing with the question of the working-class movement and the relationship of all the new forces and new alliances in this country to the working class movement and the question of political power. I think the kind of contribution that can be made by the working class in this country should be in terms of assuming a leadership role, not only in developing the alternatives to Thatcherism but in developing every aspect of our lives - not simply the question of economic exploitation but in terms of oppression; the question of women's oppression, of racial oppression, the question of ecology, of how we relate them and how we can develop those struggles together is absolutely crucial.

Peter Hain

Thanks very much Steve. I hope that the people who have disrupted this meeting so far are not going to disrupt the next speaker because he's from the steel workers and I hope that you're going to listen to him quietly for a change.

Applause

PAUL ACASTER

Brothers, sisters, comrades, I would like to bring first fraternal greetings from the steel workers and the wives and families of South Yorkshire to you tonight in solidarity.

Applause and cheering

And now you've cheered me I'm going to upset you because from what I've seen tonight the steel workers as educated trade unionists and socialists can teach you lot of people about sectarianism and solidarity because they know more about it than you do. Tony Benn was talking about reform or revolution. Well I can tell Brother Benn that because of constant attacks by successive governments, both Labour and Tory, and because of what successive Labour governments have brought about - or not brought about I should say - there are a lot of revolutionary men and women in my work place today and I know because I work there. I'm going to upset you even further. I'll tell you what my role is. I'm on the Sheffield Strike Committee and I'm in charge of fund raising and what I'm after tonight is your cash. I want your money. For Christ's sake it's so important. You know this trouble we're in today. You know what the battle is. I'm not going to insult you by telling you all about this strike, but we've got to win this brothers and sisters, you realise that. It's not just us, it's all of us and if we lose this strike then it's going to be us even further down the Swanney for Tory legislation, anti-trade union laws and the rest of it, and we've got to win this. The way you can help tonight is by getting some money: a silent collection is what I would like, whether it's taken in the hall or taken out there, and when I say silent I mean cheques and pound notes. You know how great it would be if I can go back tonight with a couple of thousand quid, if I do it right. I'll get a pat on the back when I get up there. We need this and we've got to have it to keep this strike going. And to the people who are shouting I'll say this: that if we don't win this strike they can shout now but bloody hell they'll be shouting later on. Please give us your support, we want your money.

Applause

Peter Hain

Now Sheila Rowbotham, co-author of *Beyond the Fragments*. Incidentally there will be buckets at all the doors as you go out and I ask you to give generously to the steel workers' fund.

SHEILA ROWBOTHAM

When the women's movement began we didn't begin as a non-political movement wanting women's rights, we began as a movement among some groups of women who'd been forced into a feeling that the relationships with men that we were forced to have in this kind of society were intolerable and that the ways in which we were cut off from other women were equally intolerable. We went from there and within that there are lots of differences within the women's movement. But I don't know where Tony Benn got the fact that women voted for Thatcher, because according to Eric Hobsbawm in *Marxism Today*, the groups which didn't swing to the right in the last election were women, Scots and some sections of the middle class! I think it's too simple from the point of view of feminists to divide things between rank and file tradition of resistance and simply the labourist, reformist tradition, because I think that women have had to fight within both those traditions. They've been put at the bottom of the agenda by the Labour Party and excluded even within the militant tradition of rank and file struggle because a lot of women are not working in the industries where people are very well organised. What has happened in the last ten to fifteen years is that there are thousands and thousands of socialists who don't belong to any organisation in the sense that they don't belong to a revolutionary socialist organisation or the Labour Party. They've chosen either to work within movements for autonomy like the women's movement, the gay movement, the black movement or they've chosen to work locally. One of the reasons they chose to do that was because they could not stand the way in which the left conducted itself and the way in which people who are not confident are not allowed to speak. But I think also that those of us who've been doing that also feel that it's not enough, because the situation is extremely serious. We recognise that. We're not stupid. We know that we have a state which is ultimately coercive and ultimately violent. The problem is how do people unite, how do you actually overcome the problems of real divisions and there're not just divisions between reformism and rank and file - they're divisions which are lots of different kinds of divisions, which Tony Benn illustrated in talking about some women not supporting the steel workers and some labour movement people having very sexist attitudes to women. But the problem is how do we overcome those kinds of divisions and some of us feel that we can't get the answers within the tradition of the revolutionary left nor in the reformist tradition of the Labour Party. Our experience therefore has forced us either into local organisation or organising in specific kinds of issue-orientated movements. But the problem is we need to get beyond that, and since we wrote *Beyond the Fragments* we've had a very big response from people who fairly cautiously, and with knowledge of the failures of the past of attempts to overcome those divisions, want to meet and actually discuss those things and communicate the kinds of activities in communities and in other places that people are involved in. So we are going ahead in trying to do that and we are going to have a meeting which people are very welcome to come to.

Applause

DANNY HARRIS

Danny Harris, Transport and General Workers' Union. I say that loudly. My union, unlike the fascists who are now leaving the hall, my union have fought for the rights of working people. My union have been in the forefront of the fight ...

Peter Hain

Danny hang on, hang on Danny, let them leave.

Danny Harris

... Why. Not because we shout people down at meetings, not because we're anarchist fascists, not because we believe in one party or another but because we are a union of unity of all parties across the floor. I am proud to stand here and say that I was one of the architects of defeating the social contract (or social contrick, whichever Jack Jones likes to call it) and I am pleased to say that my union was in the forefront of that fight following on from our 1977 conference when we defeated a move by the platform that the social compact should continue. But make no mistake about it - and this is where Hilary Wainwright and Paul Foot do make a mistake. The workers are not a political power as such. The workers are a mass movement and it's only within the trade union movement that you'll keep them as a mass movement because the splinter political parties will never do it. I'm also chairman of my constituency Labour Party and my Labour Party a few years ago moved its MP and we will move any MP that doesn't carry out what we, the workers, the people, want. We are proud to do that and we'll carry on doing it.

TONY SAUNOIS

Tony Saunois, Labour Party Young Socialist Representative on the National Executive Committee of the Labour Party. Comrade chairman and comrades, speaking for the youth section of the Party, we would argue and we would say that we agree with and support a lot of the ideas and statements that Tony Benn and others on the platform, particulary Stuart Holland, have advocated and put forward. We would also add differences with those comrades which we are prepared to debate and discuss in a fraternal manner. Unfortunately we do not have time tonight to outline those differences. But we would say, listening to the speech of Paul Foot, that those comrades who speak from the sectarian organisations are frankly a million light years away from the struggles of the working class and the struggles of the labour and trade union movements. Insofar as it is possible to draw any conclusions from the ideas and the speech of Paul Foot, his idea was that the Labour Party and the official trade unions are finished and they are a waste of time. That is absolute rubbish. The Labour Party was created by the working class of this country. It was Marx, Engels, Lenin and it was Trotsky who argued and pointed to the fact that the working class of this country were rooted in their traditional organisations, the trade unions. We see today a radicalisation within the Labour Party, a move towards the left, a demand for party democracy and socialist policies, a radicalisation which is a reflection of the crisis within our society. It's not a radicalisation brought about by the agitation of Paul Foot because frankly no worker in the labour and trade union movement has noticed that agitation. We've seen the radicalisation of the movement to which the marxists in the Party, the Militant tendency, have made an important contribution. And when we look at the ideas of the debate here tonight, not once do we find a programme or a policy put forward. Comrade chairman and comrades, to those workers in the audience tonight we appeal to them to join the mass organisations, the trade unions and the Labour Party and to struggle for a marxist programme, because that is is the only way forward for the working people of this country.

Peter Hain

I suppose, brothers and sisters, the only saving grace of this debate so far is that we shout at everybody in discriminately but I don't think that says very much for the ability of those on the left to talk to each other. Now Reg Race.

REG RACE

Reg Race, MP for Wood Green and speaking on behalf of the Campaign for Labour Party Democracy. I think, comrades, we all start from the assumption tonight that the last two Labour governments have been disastrous failures and that's why the Campaign for Labour Party Democracy exists because the Campaign for Labour Party Democracy believes that the two principal obstacles to real socialist change in Britain are the Parliamentary Labour Party and the TUC General

Council. The Parliamentary Labour Party is a fundamental obstacle (as it is presently constituted) to the direction of socialist change that we want to see in Britain, because it supports policies which are directly the result of pressure from the International Monetary Fund and pressure from capitalism in Britain. Clearly, if we're going to make any socialist progress in Britain we've got to make sure that the Parliamentary Labour Party is not left to its own devices but is properly and democratically accountable to the whole of the labour movement. And the first steps on that road have already been taken by the introduction of mandatory reselection that we had some fight over, in the last few years. We were defeated over the question of the election of the leader but we're going to return to that question and we've got to win that because I don't want to see Denis Healey leading the Labour Party and we have to make sure that the NEC controls the manifesto and there are many other issues that the Campaign for Labour Party Democracy wants to raise inside the Labour Party over particular issues. But we've got to make a start with the organisation of the PLP for it has sold working people out over the last two Labour governments and has implemented policies diametrically opposed to the interests of working people. And I would therefore appeal to you if you're a Labour Party supporter to support the objectives of the Campaign for Labour Party Democracy and to ensure that its policies are carried out at the next Labour Party conference.

Applause

DUNCAN HALLAS

Duncan Hallas, Socialist Workers' Party. Comrades, two minutes, two points. Tony Benn said at one point that I could just hear above the hecklers 'If the Labour Party fails then certain consequences may follow'. What

did he mean, *if* the Labour Party fails? We're not talking here comrades about some hypothesis, some untried
experiment, some new movement of which we have no
experience. For God's sake we have had seven Labour
governments, five of them, well four and a half anyway,
with a majority in parliament and indeed Brother Benn
was a cabinet minister in two of them over a con-
siderable number of years. Now, if you take the view
that the Labour Party is a socialist party - you know the
1945 Manifesto said the Labour Party is a socialist party
and proud of it - from that point of view of course we
have to say the Labour Party is an abysmal failure,
because we're talking about a record of seventy years.
But comrades, and I see the point, it would be unfair for
me to press this point too far, it would be unfair and I
don't want to be unfair because from another point of
view and a more important point of view - and that's
what really ought to concern us tonight - the Labour
Party has been a roaring success. It has been a roaring
success in terms of the ideas of those who have always
been its central leaders, from the sanctified Kier Hardie
down to the next one - I'd better not make the
suggestion - a party of reform within capitalism using
socialist rhetoric to conceal policies of reforming
capitalism. A party attempting to solve the problems of
working people, yes attempting to do so, but always
subordinated to the central priorities of capitalism. I
have little time left so I will take another quotation from
Tony Benn and I assure you I don't misrepresent him.
He said this evening 'capitalism can no longer afford
welfare'. Did he not? Did you not hear him? And then
he said also: 'The course of reform is honourable.' But
the whole course of reform comrades depends
precisely - given that you intend to operate the capitalist
system and that has been the whole history of the
Labour Party from its beginning - depends on the
possibility of the system being able to concede welfare,

being able to concede reform. I don't have to make the argument that it doesn't any more, the comrades over here agree. Now, and this is my final point, you know we are asked to believe in miracles, we are asked to believe that an institution which throughout its entire history has been an organisation of reformist conservatism - which throughout its history, although admittedly with internal conflict, has governed this country over a great many years and has preserved and sometimes strengthened British capitalism - we're asked to believe that this can become a socialist organisation. My God comrades, maybe the SWP has a hell of a hard struggle ahead of them. I don't doubt it. But at least that's the struggle of the road to a fundamental transformation of society. Their road is the road of another attempt to shore up capitalism.

Applause

ANN CESEK

I'm a member of the Labour Party and the Labour Coordinating Committee and I also support many of the ideas contained in *Socialist Challenge*. First of all, let's suppose that we win the fight for democratic change with accountability inside the Labour Party and let's also suppose that we win the fight for the Labour Party to adopt the alternative economic strategy and further-more that we're going to win the next election on that basis. What then? What are we going to do when the employers, the financial institutions and the civil service bureaucracy begins to sabotage the government's plans as they surely will and as they did in Chile? The real pro-blem is not whether you support or not but who rules: the mass movement or parliament? For who really rules the country: the unelected, privileged bureaucracy and the employers. Look what happened in 1974. It's been written in *What went Wrong?*. It's been mentioned by

Tony Benn and others - direct sabotage by Whitehall. And one more point. It's not a fanciful scare story, but if we're talking about a possible British coup, the training ground for that is in Ireland. The question we have to ask ourselves is what force is strong enough to fight against this. What the Labour leadership does is to rely upon the state and on the goodwill of the capitalists to let us come at them like thieves in the night. We have to place our faith in the labour movement alone but if we accept this conclusion, we can't go half way. We must demand not only popular participation, not power sharing, but popular sovereignty, popular power. The alternative economic strategy is an elaborate scheme to steer a wobbly course between capitalist power and popular power. It's trying to drive a car on the right and the left at the same time - like in Chile, we're all going to crash.

LYNNE SEGAL

I find it a bit absurd trying to talk here, for reasons which Sheila gave too, but I did want to try and support the arguments of Hilary and the arguments of Sheila. The main thing I want to say is that it is clear to a lot of us here, and in particular to a lot of women, that many of the most important initiatives which have happened on the left have happened both from outside of the Labour Party and from outside the revolutionary left. What's really fired people's imaginations over the last ten years has been the struggles of women, the struggles of black people, the struggles of gay people and the Irish struggles. And what I think is most important (which is a point which Hilary touched) is that if we are going to get people involved in the struggle for socialism we have to have a vision of socialism which is different from the vision of socialism which has come from the Labour Party which people see as simply more control over their lives, more bureaucratic control over their lives. So things like Lucas Aerospace, things like raising what alternatives we really want in health or in child care - all these things are absolutely crucial for the struggle for socialism. And to many of us, if we're going to actually to able to participate in revolutionary struggles, then the revolutionary organisations themselves will have to change in order to be able to incorporate us. They'll have to listen to what we've been saying over the last ten years, about what is important to us in our everyday lives and take seriously the ways in which we've been trying to organise ourselves in the community and so on. Paul Foot has made the point that power is always on the shop floor. Well it's true that that is really an important source of power. It's also unfortunately true that that's not where women are strongest at the moment. It's not inside the trade unions that women are strongest but women need to be supported from a strong autonomous women's movement from the outside, and that's what is going to help women become stronger. So therefore I think the sorts of ideas which were raised in *Beyond the Fragments* are really crucial for us all to take up and for the revolutionary left to be considering, in working out how we do organise together and how we really do try and create a mass movement which everybody feels able and confident enough to participate in. Which is able to build the confidence of everyone to be able to come up and discuss with each other - not in meetings like this which are totally alienating and almost impossible to speak in - but in other sorts of situations that we can all feel confident that there's something that we can contribute because there is something that all of us here can contribute and many of us who aren't here as well. Well I'm in a revolutionary group, *Big Flame*, which has tried to consider some of these questions and has tried to find new ways of organising which encourages the confidence of more people than has been taken seriously by the revolutionary left. I don't consider the Labour Party option a realistic option at the moment.

MONTY JOHNSTONE

Monty Johnstone, Communist Party. Comrades, there have been, I think, very many pertinent criticisms made of the present position and of the policy of the Labour Party. What has been lacking has been, it seems to me, any coherent long term strategy for the advance from where we are at the present time to the socialist objective that I think all of us in this hall agree with. And that requires, it seems to me, a recognition that it's a long haul. We have got to work out a strategy for a revolutionary process, not some coup d'etat not revolution in that sense, but in fact a revolutionary process which involves the changing of the consciousness of the people of this country. Now I disagree profoundly with the attempts to counterpose the vital importance of extra-parliamentary struggle (which has been correctly outlined by Hilary Wainwright and other comrades from the perspective of women) against a parliamentary majority for social transformation - not because I have any illusions about the character of the capitalist state which is an instrument of class oppression, but because I believe, to quote the words of Karl Marx, that it is a question of transforming universal suffrage (which incidentally was won by the working-class struggle) from a means of deception into a means of emancipation of the working class. Because I believe that any attempt to by-pass the winning of that majority will in fact lead to an authoritarian bureaucratic form of socialism. I believe also that any attempt purely to develop the organs of popular power on a local basis without paying attention to the capturing of power democratically on a national basis can only lead, firstly, to a failure adequately to confront the capitalist class where it is entrenched in control of the mechanisms of power and, secondly, even if one did succeed in getting power, it would lead to the danger of an autocratic control of the central organs of power even though one had the rights of local autonomy. Therefore I believe that what we've got to strive for is a socialist self-management, a pluralistic form of socialist democracy both on a national and on a local scale.

Applause

Peter Hain

I think we'll have to move straight on now to Tariq Ali replying for one side of the argument to be followed by Audrey Wise on the other. We have actually to be out of the hall by 10 o'clock so I aim to wind up the debate shortly before that time.

TARIQ ALI

Comrades I think it is only important that one says right at the beginning that despite the disagreement which exists between the revolutionary and reformist strands within the labour movement, debate on the central issues confronting the labour movement is absolutely vital and those who challenge the very notion of such a debate do socialism a grave disservice.

Applause

What is going to be the shape of the 1980s? That is essentially what we are discussing today. Is it going to be another tormented decade like the thirties? Are we going to tolerate a return to mass unemployment? Are we going to tolerate the politics of the 1930s - fascism conquering in Germany, the Republic defeated in Spain, a popular front in France formed supposedly to combat fascism but incapable even of aiding the destruction of fascism in Spain, a national government in Britain. That was the thirties. And when we say, or when the leaders of the TUC say 'No return to the thirties' what do they mean? I'll tell you what *we* mean. We mean that the aim of the ruling classes today and not just in Britain - Tony Benn was quite right to say that the crisis of the capitalist system is an international crisis, there is a world recession, there is an economic slump comparable to what existed in the 1930s - and in this situation we cannot for the sake of the working-class movement in Britain, Western Europe and the whole world, tolerate any return to the thirties.

It's not that what is posed is a return to fascism - I do not think that the workers' movement in Western Europe will tolerate a return to fascism. What we are seeing is in a curious way more sinister. We are seeing attempts by the ruling class today within the framework and confines of bourgeois democracy to strengthen the repressive apparatus of the state. We can see it today. We saw it on the picket lines at Hadfield not so long ago where steel pickets - not 'ultra-lefts', not revolutionary members of the IMG or the SWP but steel pickets -were brutalised by the Special Patrol Group. We have seen in Southall random brutality against ordinary black people and the murder of Blair Peach ...

Applause

... and what we say is that the repression which has been carried out by the British Army in Ireland against those striving for the unity which Tony Benn says he believes in, the repression being carried out in Ireland by the British Army will be utilised against the British working class in this country by the same army, the same officers ...

Applause

Everything indicates that the economic crisis which is a deep crisis, a fundamental crisis, means that the capitalist ruling class will turn more and more towards repression, that we will have to fight it and in the fight against that repression an organisation on the level of the factory, an organisation on the level of the neighbourhoods, building a strong revolutionary current in the labour movement to combat that repression, will be a hundred thousand times more useful than the best and most ideal of British parliaments. Tony Benn says 'we are not in favour of a coup d'etat carried out by a vanguard party'. I agree one hundred per cent. Nor are we. We are in favour of building a revolutionary party which can mobilise the majority of working people in this country to prevent a coup d'etat by the British ruling class.

Applause

You see the comrades on the other side, Tony Benn and the other brothers and sisters who support the Labour Party, face a dilemma. What is their dilemma? That they confront a situation where capitalism is in a state of advanced decay, of crisis, and where a simple tinkering with the system, a simple process of reform is not practicable within the existing framework of the capitalist economy. The ruling class knows this perfectly well. That's why they wish to change the whole mechanism by which they accumulate. That's why they wish to inflict defeat after defeat after defeat on the working-class movement. And that is why this debate is not foolish. The debate is extremely useful. I would not assume, far be it from me to assume, that we could win over Tony Benn, Audrey Wise and Stuart Holland to the ranks of a revolutionary organisation. We appeal to many of you here today who are non-aligned to participate, to join revolutionary organisations, to fight for a unified revolutionary organisation and to fight also for the right of that revolutionary organisation to seek affiliation to the Labour Party.

What is socialism? That is what the debate is about. The crisis and future of the left which can't be abstracted from what we conceive of as socialism. For me socialism is first the dissolution of the existing capitalist state and the expropriation of the ruling classes, the creation of a new type of state and economy in which the producers of wealth exercise direct control over their lives and direct power over their political representatives. That is the socialism we fight for and we say there can be no transfer of power from one social class to another until the representative apparatuses of the ruling class are broken. Because no ruling class in history, whether you go back to the revolt of the bourgeoisie against the feudal landlords - very interesting watching 'Cromwell' on television last night! - no ruling class is going to give up its power voluntarily and hence you need a new type of sovereignty which has been touched on in the debate, a popular sovereignty.

Tony says 'How can you challenge the right to vote?'' We don't challenge it. We propose a right to vote which is infinitely more democratic than the right which exists today once every five years.

Applause

We argue and we say that without this it will not be possible, that the only way socialism will be achieved is not coups d'etat carried out by vanguard parties but by winning the majority of the working people in this country to our ideas. How will they be won? Through their own experiences. And it's in the course of their experiences that it will be the task of revolutionaries to demonstrate to them that our alternative is not only correct in the abstract, it is more practical. There have been social democratic governments in Sweden, Australia, Norway, Belgium, Britain now for many many decades. Not in one single case have any of these social democratic governments brought about a fundamental shift in the relationship of class forces in favour of the working class. The one occasion on which they attempted to do so, the most left-wing government we have seen, since the seond world war, in Chile was brought down by a coup d'etat. Not by the vanguard party but by more sinister forces under the leadership of General Pinochet. And we say and we stress that it is for that reason that we believe that the Labour Party cannot deliver the goods.

A new type of party is needed, a mass revolutionary party which organises people at the point of production, which organises in the neighbourhood, which can take up all the central questions which face the working-class movement in Britain and internationally.

We don't believe that the problems of the British working class or socialism in Britain will be achieved simply in Britain, that we can isolate ourselves from the working-class movement in Western Europe, in Ireland, in other parts of the world. That is why import controls within the framework of a capitalist - existing capitalist - economy today are a utopia and they can even be a reactionary utopia as they are utilised by the extreme right to try and solve the problems which they confront at the expense of workers in France, or Italy or Spain or Portugal. That is why we reject import controls.

Applause

The comrades say that this is all left talk. This is true. I'm much happier that is is left talk rather than right talk. They say we are unrealistic. Which revolutionary hypothesis has been realistic in situations of normality anywhere in the world? In the first instance all revolutionary hypotheses appear unrealistic. They become practical when the consciousness of the working class reaches a pitch where it looks for new solutions and these solutions cannot simply be provided by parliament. They need new forms of organisation, new types of structures and more democracy. Tony says there are two pillars of strength. Unity and parliament - unity? Yes! Unity in action against racism? Yes! Unity in action against the Tory government? Yes! Unity in action against unemployment? Yes! Unity in action against the cuts? Yes! Unity in action against the Corrie

Bill? Yes! Unity so that we dissolve our politics? No!

Applause

And the second pillar is parliament. Tony talked about the Chartists. You know many of the demands of the Chartists have yet to be fulfilled. You know that. And they won't be fulfilled by this ruling class. There is an old story - an Arab legend about a merchant in Baghdad with his servant and his servant suddenly meets Death in the market place and to escape from Death he hurries off and takes the road to Samara. The merchant is very cross that he has lost his servant and says - he confronts Death and says: "Why did you frighten my servant?" "I didn't just mean to frighten him," says Death. "I really didn't. It's just that I was surprised to see him in Baghdad for I have an appointment with him in Samara tonight". Comrades, we do not wish the labour movement in Britain to take the road to Samara. And that is why we are opposed to Labourism, that weak, sickly and pathetic ideology which has dominated the British working class. It must be displaced if we are to move forward.

Applause

Peter Hain

Now Audrey Wise who was until the last election, MP for Coventry South West and is vice chairman of the Labour Coordinating Committee. Audrey.

AUDREY WISE

Comrades. Paul Foot said that those who have power will not cede it willingly. And he is probably right. He said 'They will try to shoot the opposition' or words to that effect. 'They will shoot the opposition.' Right. But a question arises here comrades. Does that mean that the chairmen of the multinationals who grow fat on their huge salaries will actually be firing the guns? No, I think we'd agree, it doesn't mean that. It means that they will rely on ordinary people either to do it for them or to acquiesce while it is done.

Interruption - 'The state, you fool'

The trouble is I don't believe that the state is some sort of abstraction. I believe that the state itself depends on acquiescence at least, if not support from ordinary people. And so the big question to which we've got to find the answer is how to persuade ordinary people not to acquiesce while they are prevented from achieving the transfer of wealth and power towards themselves. What we are really talking about comrades, brothers and sisters, ladies and gentlemen and others, what we are talking about is how to increase and awaken socialist consciousness. That's what it is about. Now when I fought to be elected to parliament I said in my election addresses 'Big business rules Britain' and I'll stand by that. But by God, they get a great deal of cooperation from parliament and from government and from the civil service and they would have a great deal harder job to rule Britain without that cooperation.

Our friends here tell us that parliament is impotent. Paul said: 'Go where the power is, not in parliament, not in trade union offices, but on the shop floor.' But then later on he says: 'Let's unite in action against the Union Bill, against the cuts.' Where does he think they emanate from then? Heaven? Of course not. From that place over there! Years ago *Socialist Worker* described parliament as a corpse. Well I reckon it's a corpse with a very active trigger finger and it's been doing a lot of damage in the years which have elapsed since they described it as a corpse.

I'm not suggesting that we give pats on the head, Hilary, to extra-parliamentary activity. I think that some of us do a great deal more than that. I think that some of us realise that there is not a conflict, there is no God who says: 'You can only be in parliament and you cannot be on the Grunwick picket line.' If there is such a God he doesn't work with all of us!

And does it not strengthen workers' struggles if they have some voices raised in parliament, elected by their own votes, to *support* them for a change? Does that not strengthen their struggle?

Paul Foot says that it's only when Labour governments falter and fall that we welcome people on the streets. Was he not in Hyde Park when the Chairman of the Labour Party spoke on behalf of the Fire Brigades Union, then locked in combat with the Labour government? Does he not recognise that the really interesting and important arena of struggle in this country is in fact the labour movement itself? Does he not realise the job that was done in exposing one of the very many Tories in our ranks by Newham North East Labour Party? Who got rid of Reg Prentice? Not the SWP. Not the IMG. But a constituency Labour Party. Wasn't that worth doing?

We are the heirs, we're not the originators, of struggle in this country. We're the heirs of generations who have been fighting to improve the lot of working people. Hilary talked about Tyneside. I've got a long tradition in my family on Tyneside. I can tell Hilary, unfortunately, Tyneside has not been the stronghold of socialism, it has been the stronghold of the wrong sort of Labourism and is to this day in many of its manifestations. It's no use our thinking that there was a golden age or that there is a magic path.

I am not willing to say to the suffragettes that they are wrong. I think I'd have been a suffragette (if I'd had the courage) and wouldn't you? Wouldn't you have been a Chartist? What about in Rhodesia where they have been fighting a war, a war which has culminated in achieving the right to elect a government, a good deal less perfect in fact than the right that we have. The Rhodesian constitution is very imperfect indeed but they regard it as an opportunity to advance on their previous struggles. And if you were a South African would you not be fighting for the right to vote for a parliament if you were a black. Of course you would, of course they are. So are we to say that we will leave that place over there to do its damndest on the working class while we pretend it doesn't exist?

There is no conflict between struggle outside and inside parliament except the conflict which is created by those who betray the struggle and you can betray it outside and inside. You don't have to go to parliament to betray. So alright we haven't won yet and they haven't won in Sweden and Norway etc. etc. etc. Alright, none of us have won yet, neither those who advocate the lines put by Paul Foot and Tariq Ali nor those on this side, none of us have won. We can agree on that can't we, it's self evident. Does that mean that we can draw empty conclusions that the efforts are to no avail? Of course it doesn't. Nearly every speaker on this platform has talked about the Corrie Bill. Hilary said that parliament was marginal in the defeat of the Corrie Bill. That it depended on the activity of women outside. Of course it depended on the activities of women outside, of course it did, but did they not need a few people going into the division lobby? Did they not? Did they manage it by magic?

I don't believe in magic, I don't believe in faith, I don't ask you to have faith in the Labour Party. I believe in the power of reason and love and that is what politics is about - not faith. But reason demands that you look at the Labour Party and realise that it has within it the efforts of countless ordinary working people and I am not willing to retire from that struggle and leave that party to Jim Callaghan.

Applause

That's the gospel of defeatism and when it comes down to it they don't actually want us to. Tariq Ali says: 'Get the Labour Party in such a democratic state that it will accept affiliation from the IMG. He says to us: 'Do that colossal task, democratise the party', and we know it's a big task, we've been trying. And we are winning. That is why there is such panic in the breasts of the right wing. That's why they are now all embracing 'super democracy', everybody has a vote (especially *The Sun* newspaper) in the reselection of MPs. The right wing is panicking, because the left is advancing in the Labour Party. But I must tell Tariq. You know, without the help of a few more people I doubt, well let's say I think it'll take rather a long time for us to get to the stage where we can say 'O.K. we have won to such an extent that the IMG can affiliate'. Then they would come along and help us. Big deal. Big deal.

Applause

So let's realise that there are things to be done in awakening socialist consciousness but that an important bit of socialist consciousness is contained in the Labour Party constitution which talks about common owner-ship of the means of production, distribution and exchange. And despite their efforts they haven't got rid of that have they? Despite their efforts. We have the Labour Party constitution as a basis, and we have the work which has been done, but we have a great deal more, of course, to do. Of course, we know that, that's no news.

Awakening socialist consciousness involves show-ing people that electing a Labour government is about achieving an economic democracy as well as a political democracy, so that people will work to produce useful goods like outlined in the Lucas workers' plan. Hilary knows, the Lucas workers didn't scorn to try to get our help in parliament! The Lucas workers knew that a

Labour government could have been the means of putting flesh on their plan. Labour governments haven't simply failed, Labour governments have refused to try to use parliament. Labour governments have refused to carry out Clause 4 of the Labour Party constitution. But it wasn't compulsory that they did that; they did that, brothers and sisters, because we all allowed them to get away with it.

I believe in struggle on the streets. Incidentally Paul Foot says 'Industrial, not geographical'. If you said community instead of geography would that sound better? I object, I object to defining the struggle as though it only goes on in factories. It goes on in homes, it goes on in ...

Applause

... it goes on in housing estates and blocks of flats and factories, and offices, and schools, and hospitals - and in parliament. And in parliament! I am not appealing for people here to join the Labour Party. But I hope that when they have occasion to join an anti-cuts campaign or to go on strike or engage in any other forms of activity, I hope that they will learn the lesson of the fact that at least some of their energy will be directed towards altering what happens in parliament.

Even Paul Foot, when they had a little bit of difficulty at *Socialist Worker*, came to parliament and said 'Please can you promote a Private Members' Bill' forsooth. Even I thought that showed a few illusions in parliament!

So it's not for or against parliament, it's for or against struggle using all the institutions which we have and which we need to create, that's what it's all about comrades.

Applause

Peter Hain

Thank you Audrey. We've got a few important announcements before you leave. First of all please give generously to the steel strikers' fund. Secondly on behalf of the friends of Blair Peach Committee there's a national demonstration on the 27 April and the reopening of the inquest on 28 April and it's important that that is supported. If anybody wants to buy the record of this debate, certain interruptions deleted, then would they put their cheques and their order forms in the box outside. There are a number of other announcements which I don't have time for but would you please leave the hall as quickly as you can as we're due to be out of here by ten o'clock. Thanks very much.

The Debate of the Decade

A 90 minute cassette containing the highlight of the debate has been specially produced by the Labour Coordinating Committee. A unique record of the event and therefore of interest in itself, the cassette is aimed for use at local socialist meetings, to provoke discussion.

Available from the Labour Coordinating Committee, price £1.99 plus 50p post and packing each, from 9 Poland Street, London W1 (discounts available on orders of 20 or more: phone 01-439 4379).